HOW-TO SERIES

SERVE
YOUR
CITY

HOW TO DO IT AND WHY IT MATTERS

SMALL GROUP
LEADER'S GUIDE

ISBN: 9781642960013

Published by ARC, The Association of Related Churches

Printed in the United States

TABLE
OF CONTENTS

4 | WEEK 1
Connect with the Heart of God

12 | WEEK 2
Discover Your Serve

22 | WEEK 3
Crack the Code of Your Community

30 | WEEK 4
Build the Culture

40 | WEEK 5
Plan the Serve

50 | WEEK 6
Lead the Serve

58 | WEEK 7
Next Steps: Show & Tell

66 | ANSWER KEY

69 | RESOURCES

71 | ABOUT ARC

WEEK ONE

CONNECT WITH THE HEART OF GOD

OPENING

Begin by opening up with prayer. Review Introduction and give the group an idea of what the semester will look like.

ICEBREAKER

TAKE CARE: Read the following quiz to your group. Tell them they don't have to answer, just ponder.

1. Who are the five wealthiest people in the world?
2. Name five winners of the Academy Award.

Now, read the next set of questions to them:

1. Name five people who have influenced you in a positive way.

2. Name five people who have brought you joy or made you feel cared for.

Point: The lesson is obvious—on a personal level, fame, wealth, and achievement pale in comparison to care and compassion.

MAIN FOCUS

People will forget what we say or do but they will remember how we made them feel. Our actions toward others should convey the love of Jesus in a way that it makes them want all that He has to offer.

SHOW & TELL

Allow participants time to discuss the questions from this week's session. Discuss the Show & Tell section. At the end, explain what the group can expect next week.

PRAYER FOCUS

God, help us to be more aware of how our words and actions can point others to You.

COLOSSIANS 1:27

Christ, the anointed One and His anointing, is in me. He is my hope and expectations of glory.

CONNECT WITH THE HEART OF GOD

The ability to truly love and serve others comes out of the overflow of our abiding relationship with Jesus Christ. When loving and serving others is the overflow of Christ's life in us, then our Serve comes out of abundance. We must first understand that, as believers, Christ is living in us. We are not serving and loving people for Jesus but rather with Him.

When you love someone, you learned to love the things they love. Serving people in need through simple acts of kindness is an outward expression of our love for God and for people. Our care for others has the ability to open the hearts of those being served (as well as those who are serving) to the love of Jesus. It also connects our hearts to the thing closest to God's heart: people.

Jesus gave us the two greatest commandments. The first is to love God and the second is to love people. (Matthew 22:36-40) We can live out both of these commandments through serving others.

MATTHEW 25:35-40 ESV

"For I was hungry and you gave me food, I was thirsty and you gave me drink, I was a stranger and you welcomed me, I was naked and you clothed me, I was sick and you visited me, I was in prison and you came to me.' Then the righteous will answer him, saying, 'Lord, when did we see you hungry and feed you, or thirsty and give you drink? And when did we see you a stranger and welcome you, or naked and clothe you? And when did we see you sick or in prison and visit you?' And the King will answer them, 'Truly, I say to you, as you did it to one of the least of these my brothers, you did it to me.'"

Serving others should point to **GOD**, not self.

Serving others should be a vehicle to **FORM RELATIONSHIPS** with others so that they may come to know Jesus personally.

Serving others should be a **SAMPLE** of the gospel of Jesus Christ.

Serving others should go the **EXTRA MILE** to show others God's love. (Matthew 5:41)

Serving others will **GLORIFY** God through His church. (Matthew 5:16)

From what we see in Jesus' life and ministry, God has called us to *show* the love of God as we *tell* people about Him. Throughout this study, we'll look at ways we can follow Jesus' example.

TELL IT

In what ways can your life point people to God?

....

....

....

....

....

How can you allow others to sample Jesus?

....

....

....

....

....

Explain a time where you have gone the extra mile for someone. What did it mean to him or her, and what did it mean for you?

....

....

....

....

....

....

What are some tangible, concrete ways God can be glorified through your life?

....

....

....

....

....

....

SHOW IT

This week, "Go the Extra Mile." When others ask you to do something for them, don't simply do it—take it one step further. Whatever you do, big or small, do it in a way that points back to God. Ask the questions, "What would Jesus do, and how would He do it?"

A FEW OF MY THOUGHTS...

....

....

....

....

....

....

....

....

....

....

....

....

....

....

....

....

....

....

....

....

....

....

....

....

....

WEEK TWO
DISCOVER YOUR SERVE

REFLECTION

Begin the group with prayer. Allow time to discuss the previous week's Show & Tell.

ICEBREAKER

I CAN...

Aim: To get people to thinking about their abilities, gifts and talents and the gifts and talents of others.

Activity: Get the group to think of two skills they have. Allow a few minutes for people to think.

Each person takes a turn to share their talents. Go around the group and have each person say, "I can . . ." Complete the sentence with two things they feel they're good at doing.

> **Example:** *I can paint and I can pray.*

MAIN FOCUS

We are all God's handiwork who have been created for a special purpose. God made each of us the way He wanted, with a specific role so that we can care for each other.
(Read 1 Corinthians 12:12-31.)

SHOW & TELL

Allow participants time to discuss the questions from this week's session. Encourage your group to complete any spiritual gifts test or personality test your church offers. Also, encourage them to complete any steps that you church has in place for assimilation. You can also point them to some online assessments and do them together as a group.

Spiritual Gifts: **http://www.spiritualgiftstest.com/test/adult**

ARC Personality profile: **https://www.arcchurches.com/disc/**

PRAYER FOCUS

Lord, show us how our gifts and personality have been uniquely created and how we can use it to edify the body of Christ.

1 PETER 4:10-11 ESV

As each has received a gift, use it to serve one another, as good stewards of God's varied grace: whoever speaks, as one who speaks oracles of God; whoever serves, as one who serves by the strength that God supplies—in order that in everything God may be glorified through Jesus Christ. To him belong glory and dominion forever and ever. Amen.

WEEK TWO

DISCOVER YOUR SERVE

Serving others and building a culture of serving begins with you. Every person is uniquely created for a specific purpose. In order to discover our Serve, we need to understand how God made us.

THE CORE OF WHO YOU ARE

SPIRITUAL GIFTS : God equips you with gifts to fulfill the purpose He created you to accomplish.

HEART and **PASSION** : What touches your heart? What people capture your attention? What activities are you constantly gravitating toward? Where are you already spending your time, money and energy?

ABILITIES : Your abilities and talents are tools in the hands of God to fulfill His purposes. (Ephesians 2:10)

PERSONALITY : Your personality type is one of the ways God has equipped you to do what you were created to do.

EXPERIENCES : Whether they are pleasant or painful (family, educational, career, etc.), God can use your difficult experiences as much as the good ones. Turn your pain into purpose.

DISCOVERING YOURSELF AND YOUR PURPOSE

SPIRITUAL GIFTS ASSESSMENT: Take a spiritual gift assessment. See if your church has an assessment available or take this one online: **www.spiritualgiftstest.com/spiritual-gifts-test-adult-version**

PERSONALITY TYPE: Understanding how God has wired you can be a big clue to your purpose. Understanding personality types can help us understand how we influence others on our teams or in our groups. **www.arcchurches.com/disc**

NOTICE THE THEMES: What are the types of people, topics and activities that you tend to gravitate toward?

BE STILL: Take time to be quiet and hear God speak.

EXPERIMENT: Explore and engage in different activities. You may not find your passion immediately, but it is a way to get started.

EXAMPLES OF SPIRITUAL GIFTS AND HOW THEY CAN BE USED TO SERVE:

ADMINISTRATION The gift of organizational skills	*Planning and organizing details for Serves, preparing emails and other communications for Serve events.*
CRAFTSMANSHIP The gift to plan, build and work with your hands	*Handyman repair work for widows, building wheelchair ramps for the disabled, teaching skills to young men.*
EVANGELISM The gift to help non-Christians take the steps to becoming born again	*This gift can be used in virtually any project or Serve setting where we are reaching others.*
EXHORTATION The gift to encourage others	*Coach an Outreach Small Group.*
HEALING The gift of prayer & laying on of hands for divine healing	*Visit nursing homes or hospitals and pray for the elderly and sick.*

EXAMPLES OF SPIRITUAL GIFTS AND HOW THEY CAN BE USED TO SERVE:

HELPS The gift to support and assist others	*Support a teacher/classroom in a school, Serve as administrative support for a local ministry.*
HOSPITALITY The gift to create a warm, welcoming environment for others	*Feed the homeless, take meals to shut-ins, Serve those serving, or host a small group in your home.*
INTERCESSION The gift to stand in the gap in prayer and believe God for results	*Lead a prayer walk over neighborhoods, schools and city.*
LEADERSHIP The gift to influence people at their level by casting vision	*Lead an outreach small group that is meeting a need in the community.*
MERCY The gift to feel empathy and care for those hurting	*Serve as a volunteer in a hospital or nursing home.*
MISSIONARY The gift to reach others outside your culture	*Welcome and acclimate International Exchange Students. Lead short term mission trips.*

SHOW
AND
TELL

TELL IT

When volunteering in the past, in what roles did you each find your-self serving? Were you comfortable in the role? Why or why not?

....

....

....

....

....

....

Talk about how the different personality types interact with each other. Which ones interact easily? Which ones create friction?

....

....

....

....

....

....

What are you naturally good at doing?

....

....

....

....

....

As you think about your team or group, how do your different personalities, gifts and talents complement each other? Can you see that God has uniquely equipped each of you, and collectively, your gifts can accomplish far more than any individual could do?

....

....

....

....

....

SHOW IT

1 Have a conversation with one person (your spouse, a good friend, or a group member) and talk about how you can use your experiences, personality, talents, and spiritual gifts more effectively to serve others?

2 After this conversation, ask God for one clear step you can take to serve.

3 Take that step.

A FEW OF MY THOUGHTS...

WEEK THREE

CRACK THE CODE OF YOUR COMMUNITY

REFLECTION

Begin the group with prayer. Allow time to discuss the previous week's Show & Tell. Ask, "What did you learn about yourself?"

ICEBREAKER

Allow each person in the group tell how long they have lived in your specific community and describe their experience when they first moved to the community.

After sharing, note the differences between group's members who have lived in the community a long time and those newer to the community. Discuss with the group the obvious changes that have taken place in the community and the impact on the people.

MAIN FOCUS

In order to serve a community, you must first know the community and understand the different needs of the people living there.

Read: "And let us consider how to stir up one another to love and good works," Hebrews 10:24 ESV

SHOW & TELL

Give the group time for the "Tell It" portion of the Show & Tell. Allow them to share and compare notes on the individuals and ministries they each came up with. Compile a list of the needs that were identified, and together, decide on which needs are the greatest of the community. Discuss the individuals and resources that were identified and potential ways the group could utilize those to help meet a need. Explain the importance of the "Show It" portion and how their commitment to follow through can help them as a group succeed in knowing how to help the community.

PRAYER FOCUS

Lord, give us insight into our city, community and neighborhoods so that we can fully understand the needs. Help us to see how You have equipped us to meet those needs in order to show Your love to those who have yet to come to know You.

HEBREWS 10:24-25 ESV

And let us consider how to stir up one another to love and good works, not neglecting to meet together, as is the habit of some, but encouraging one another, and all the more as you see the Day drawing near.

WEEK THREE
CRACK THE CODE OF YOUR COMMUNITY

We crack the code in our communities by having intentional (and sometimes spontaneous) conversations . . . and listening very carefully. In most cases, the people who are already in our churches know the code. They haven't told us only because we haven't asked.

KNOW YOUR PEOPLE

IDENTIFY and **ENGAGE** the people within your church who serve or are connected with local ministries or agencies that are already serving the community. As a leader your job is to connect with the body and know all the parts of the body and their function.

Now there are varieties of gifts, but the same Spirit; and there are varieties of service, but the same Lord; and there are varieties of activities, but it is the same God who empowers them all in everyone. To each is given the manifestation of the Spirit for the common good. . . . All these are empowered by one and the same Spirit, who apportions to each one individually as he wills. (1 Corinthians 12:4–7, 11 ESV)

KNOW YOUR COMMUNITY

Discover the **NEEDS** of the community. Look at demographic data, talk to local officials, law enforcement, ministries and local agencies leaders to gain a greater perspective of the true felt needs of the community.

Let each of you look not only to his own interests, but also to the interests of others. (Philippians 2:4)

KNOW YOUR RESOURCES

Leverage the **RESOURCES** already available in the community. Don't waste resources recreating something that God has already provided. We can be good stewards by utilizing the resources that are already available to us.

"And he who had received the five talents came forward, bringing five talents more, saying, 'Master, you delivered to me five talents; here I have made five talents more.' His master said to him, 'Well done, good and faithful servant. You have been faithful over a little; I will set you over much. Enter into the joy of your master.'" (Matthew 25:20-21)

TELL IT

Write down and share with the group three people that you know in the church who are already serving or connected with a local ministry or social agency.

....

....

....

....

....

....

Discuss with your group the obvious needs you see in the community.

....

....

....

....

....

....

Identify some individuals, local ministries or agencies that are providing valuable resources that are underutilized and under-supported.

....

....

....

....

....

....

SHOW IT ▰▬▬▬▬

This week be intentional to connect over lunch or coffee with a person in the church or one of the organizations that were identified. Be prepared to give your group a summary of your meeting.

A FEW OF MY THOUGHTS...

WEEK FOUR

BUILD THE CULTURE

REFLECTION

Begin with prayer. Allow time for participants to discuss the previous week's Serve challenge. You can start the discussion by sharing your own experience of "going the extra mile."

ICEBREAKER

Have the participants write down "salt" and "light" and the three attributes of each that are listed below. Have the group come up with ways they can be salt and light.

SALT	LIGHT
Heals	Removes Darkness
Preserves	Illuminates the Way
Enhances Flavor	Causes Growth

MAIN FOCUS

Life change happens within the context of relationships. We have the ability to shape our society and culture by being salt and light in our sphere of influence. We do this through the relationships we establish when we serve others.

SHOW & TELL

Allow participants time to discuss the questions from this week's session. Discuss ways the group can complete the Show & Tell of being salt and light in their environments this week.

PRAYER FOCUS

Lord, help us to be vessels that facilitate love, growth, truth, excellence, vision and healing to those around us.

MATTHEW 5:13-16 NKJV

"You are the salt of the earth; but if the salt loses its flavor, how shall it be seasoned? It is then good for nothing but to be thrown out and trampled underfoot by men. You are the light of the world. A city that is set on a hill cannot be hidden. Nor do they light a lamp and put it under a basket, but on a lampstand, and it gives light to all who are in the house. Let your light so shine before men, that they may see your good works and glorify your Father in heaven."

WEEK FOUR
BUILD THE CULTURE

Our culture is shaped by our relationships and lifestyle. As Christians we are called to be the salt of the earth and light in a dark world. We have the ability to bring flavor and warmth into the world by loving and serving others each day. Having a church culture of serving begins with us.

LIFESTYLE

FIVE TRUTHS DEFINE AND SHAPE A CULTURE OF SERVING:

1. As believers, serving is our **MANDATE**. (Galatians 5:13-14)

2. Serving is about **PEOPLE**, no matter where they are. (Philippians 2:3)

3. Help others become **OVERCOMERS** . (1 Thessalonians 5:11)

4. Build the **LOCAL CHURCH** . (Ephesians 4:12)

5. Remember the **POOR** . (Deuteronomy 15:11) *We define the "poor" as anyone in any kind of bondage or under any kind of oppression who needs to experience the freedom of Christ.*

RELATIONSHIPS

A culture is built on relationships because life change happens in the context of relationships. Small groups provide the place for us to build relationships and serve together. Within these relationships, we can learn to be the salt and light of the world.

> The one who plants and the one who waters work as a team with the same purpose. (1 Corinthians 3:8 NLT)

FOUR T.E.A.M. COMPONENTS OF HEALTHY RELATIONSHIPS:

(1) TRUST : Many people claim to be loyal, but it is hard to find a trustworthy person. (Proverbs 20:6 NCV)

- Be **CONSISTENT** : Whoever can be trusted with very little can also be trusted with much. (Luke 16:10 NIV)

- Be **CONFIDENTIAL** : A gossip betrays a confidence, but a trustworthy man keeps a secret. (Proverbs 11:13 NIV)

- Be **CLOSE** : Friends love through all kinds of weather, and families stick together in all kinds of trouble. (Proverbs 17:17 MSG)

(2) **EMPATHY** : Live in harmony with one another; be sympathetic. (1 Peter 3:8 NIV)

- **SLOW DOWN** : Be quick to listen and slow to speak... (James 1:19 NIV)

- Ask **QUESTIONS** : The purposes of a man's heart are deep waters, but a man of understanding draws them out. (Proverbs 20:5 NIV)

- Show **YOUR EMOTIONS** : Rejoice with those who rejoice; mourn with those who mourn. (Romans 12:15 NIV)

(3) **ACCOMMODATE** : Be faithful, loving, and easy to get along with. (2 Timothy 2:22 CEV)

- Each other's **NEEDS** : Each one of us needs to look after the good of the people around us, asking ourselves, "How can I help?" (Romans 15:2 MSG)

- Each other's **IDEAS** : The intelligent man is always open to new ideas. In fact, he looks for them. (Proverbs 18:15 LB)

- Each other's **PERSONALITIES** : We have different gifts, according to the grace given us. (Romans 12:6 NIV)

- Each other's **FAULTS** : Be completely humble and gentle; be patient, bearing with one another in love. (Ephesians 4:2 NIV)

(4) **MISSION** : Live in a way that brings honor to the Good News of Christ...standing strong with one purpose, working together as one for the faith of the Good News. (Philippians 1:27 NCV)

- Set **GOALS** as a group.

- Establish your group's **WIN** .

- Know each other's **STRENGTHS** and **WEAKNESSES** .

- Assign **ROLES** and **TASKS** .

TELL IT

Share a time when you were the salt and light in a situation. What were the results?

....

....

....

....

....

....

Share how you are shaping (or want to shape) a culture of being salt and light in your home, school, work or community.

....

....

....

....

....

....

Discuss why each of the T.E.A.M. components are important when serving together.

....

....

....

....

....

....

SHOW IT ▰▬▬▬▰

Serving is contagious. This week identify a simple way your group can serve someone in your sphere of influence. It can be a friend, family member or the local bank teller. Your Serve can be something as simple as taking the local fire department a fresh baked pan of muffins.

The important thing is to be intentional about incorporating this week's thoughts into your Serve. Take note of how your groups works together.

Check out our website for ideas at
www.showandtellthebook.com.

A FEW OF MY THOUGHTS...

WEEK FIVE

PLAN THE SERVE

REFLECTION

Allow time to discuss the previous week's challenge. Share experiences of sharing your story of faith and how it was received.

ICEBREAKER

A day or two before the group meets, tell one participant to select half the group, plan and organize them to build a platform that will hold a cell phone in a vertical position.

As the group begins, divide them into two teams—one of which is already identified and organized. Provide an adequate supply of objects like Legos, blocks, paperclips, etc. that the teams can choose to use for building. Instruct the teams to build a platform that will hold an object (but don't tell the second team how the platform will be used, and if they ask, don't tell them). Give them five minutes to construct the platform, and then ask them to stop. Now reveal to the second team that they are to use their platform to hold a cell phone in a vertical position.

Obviously, the team who planned ahead was able to strategize and organize, choosing the right materials and constructing the platform for the purpose it was intended.

MAIN FOCUS

Excellence inspires people and honors God. We are to give God our best and that requires us to plan and be prepared.

SHOW & TELL

Allow participants time to discuss the questions from this week's session. Also, as a group, plan a simple Serve that you can do together at the next meeting.

PRAYER FOCUS

Lord, help us show honor to You by serving with excellence so that we inspire others to give their lives to You.

PROVERBS 16:3 ESV

Commit your work to the Lord, and your plans will be established.

WEEK FIVE
PLAN THE SERVE

Over the past few weeks, we have focused on understanding the heart of God, discovering our gifts, cracking the code of our community and creating a culture of serving. Now we're ready to put what we've learned into action: we'll plan a practical way to serve our community.

PRAY FIRST

Your planning should begin with fervent, heart-felt prayer. Prayer is the key to leading people to Christ and is essential to seeing lives changed.

> The earnest prayer of a righteous person has great power and produces wonderful results. (James 5:16 NLT)

OUTREACH SERVE IDEAS

As we have seen in this study, your gifts and passions should help you determine how you serve. Other areas that you should consider are the felt needs of the community that you identified. "Felt needs" are changes deemed necessary to correct the deficiencies you perceive in the community.

PLANNING THE SERVE

Review the information from your meetings with people in the church and with local ministries. What needs of the community have you uncovered? Consider the needs and your group's gifting and available resources. This analysis should help you determine what God has already equipped you to do, and then, choose the need your group wants to meet. Once you have an idea of how and where you want to serve, there are several areas to take into consideration:

- ✓ **PARTICIPANTS:** Protection for those serving, skills needed, volunteers needed, role assignment.

- ✓ **RECIPIENTS:** Hearts to be opened of those being served.

- ✓ **FINANCIAL:** Budget (materials, equipment & rentals, promotional, shirts, food, signage, margin).

- ✓ **PLANNING:** Team & process, checklist & timeline.

- ✓ **SERVES:** Scope (know your limits) & location.

✓ **PARTNERS**: Ministries & resources that you can come along side and further their efforts.

✓ **COMMUNICATION**: Is everyone on the same page? (leaders, participants and recipients)

✓ **RESOURCES**: There are many things you can do that don't even require a budget.

- **Donations:** Vendors that may donate materials or services.

- **People:** Members that may have talents/assets to lend to serving. Let your people be the "wow factor." People may forget what you said and did, but they will remember how you made them feel.

- **Serve Costs:** Materials and supplies.

ADDITIONAL CONSIDERATIONS

FREQUENCY: Will you be doing this Serve on a consistent basis? (Weekly, monthly etc.) Is this something you can sustain long-term?

SERVE DATE AND LOCATION: Are there other events or holidays on or close to your chosen date that may conflict with your Serve? Are there events with which you need to coordinate your event?

ORGANIZE YOUR TEAM: Make sure all of those involved understand their roles and are being utilized to their full potential. Communicate deadlines. Organize members in pairs or groups so that there is more than one person responsible for a specific task.

OBTAIN CLEARANCE: Prior to the Serve date, obtain permissions from local authorities, property owners, community leaders, etc. that may be required.

RISK MANAGEMENT: Assess possible safety concerns, and put measures in place that can mitigate any concerns.

DOCUMENT: Throughout the planning and execution of the Serve, keep a journal of what worked, what didn't and what could have been done better.

TELL IT

Discuss the Big Win. How can others experience Jesus through your Serve?

....

....

....

....

....

....

....

....

....

....

....

....

....

....

....

Discuss the challenges your team faced in the planning process. How did the process draw you closer together?

....

....

....

....

....

....

....

....

....

....

....

....

....

....

SHOW IT

As a group, come up with a Serve that incorporates your group's skills, passions, and resources that will meet a felt need in the community. Then, plan the Serve incorporating all of the thoughts from this week's discussion. (Keep it simple.) The planning process is where those in the group with the attention for details get to shine.

A FEW OF MY THOUGHTS...

WEEK SIX

LEAD THE SERVE

REFLECTION

This week you will review the plans you made last week and execute the Serve. Make sure everyone understands the vision of the Serve. What is the win? Does everyone know their role in the Serve? Is there an order or a timeframe that needs to be followed? Remind everyone to incorporate into the Serve all the other things they have learned over the last few weeks.

ICEBREAKER

In this activity, people are asked to interact to discover their hidden role. You'll need one sticky note per person. Before the group meets, write a different job or role on each note, for instance: fireman, nurse, astronaut, pastor, plumber, accountant, mason, farmer, etc. Make sure there are no duplicates.

When the group meets, place a sticky note on the back or forehead of each person. Don't let them see what's written on it! Their task is to figure out what role is written on their notes.

Give them these instructions: Find a partner and silently read your partner's note. You can ask each other three questions, but you can answer only "yes" or "no." After each of you have asked the three questions, make a guess what's written on your note. If your partner says you're right, move your note to your chest, and you can become a "consultant" who gives clues to others about good questions they might ask. If you guess wrong, find a new partner and ask three questions again. Repeat this until you get it right.

MAIN FOCUS

We are the hands and feet of Jesus. It is through us that Jesus can touch the lives of others. As His ambassadors, we should work together with all our heart as though we are working for the Lord.

SHOW & TELL

Challenge participants to go home and journal about the Serve experience. What were the wins? What could have been done better? How did it make them feel?

PRAYER FOCUS

Lord, help us to serve with excellence so that we can bring honor and glory to Your name.

PROVERBS 29:18 KJV

Where there is no vision, the people perish: but
he that keepeth the law, happy is he.

WEEK SIX
LEAD THE SERVE

The success of a plan doesn't stop with the planning. The implementation is just as important. There are three key elements we should include when implementing a Serve.

 Share the **VISION** .

We get to be the hands and feet of Jesus. We serve others in practical ways so that they may become fully devoted followers of Christ.

2 Know your team and the **ROLES** .

It's not enough to have people in your group. You need the right people in the right roles. First, you must know your team and their strengths. Second, you need to know the specific roles needed for the Serve. Match strengths to the appropriate roles.

> ...from whom the whole body, joined and held together by every joint with which it is equipped, when each part is working properly, makes the body grow so that it builds itself up in love. (Ephesians 4:16 ESV)

Consider outlining on paper the people involved in the Serve and what their roles will be in your overall plan of action. We are wired to work, but to work with a purpose. Outlining everyone's role in the Serve will help keep the group accountable and ensure that everyone is contributing to the shared vision.

3 Have a **TIMELINE** .

Establishing a clear timeline can help you Serve successfully. Everyone needs to know when to start and when the Serve is to be complete.

> But all things should be done decently and in order. (1 Corinthians 14:40 ESV)

TELL IT

Recall a project or activity you've been a part of where the vision was clear and roles were defined. How did it positively affect your experience? What did you learn from it?

....

....

....

....

....

....

God has gifted us all differently. Discuss with the group where each person can contribute.

....

....

....

....

....

....

Discuss the timeline of your Serve and what the group thinks needs to take place.

....

....

....

....

....

....

....

....

....

....

....

....

SHOW IT

Here's the challenge: As a group, review your plan to Serve. Discuss and agree on what the "big wins" should be. Discuss each person's role for the Serve and the expected timeline. Execute the Serve.

A FEW OF MY THOUGHTS...

....

....

....

....

....

....

....

....

....

....

....

....

....

....

....

....

....

....

....

....

....

....

....

....

WEEK SEVEN

NEXT STEPS: SHOW & TELL

REFLECTION

Allow time to discuss the previous week's Serve. Have the participants share their thoughts on the wins, ways it could improve and what they learned from the experience.

ICEBREAKER

Go around the room and let each person share what gifts and talents they feel God has revealed that they can use to serve others and where they feel God is directing them to serve.

MAIN FOCUS

God has equipped you for a purpose. Your spiritual gifts and passions form the unique way God has wired you to serve.

SHOW & TELL

Allow participants to ask questions about serving, and perhaps, leading an Outreach small group. Discuss how leading a small group can allow them to connect with others who share their interests and passions. Make sure they know when and where the next available small group leadership training will be held.

PRAYER FOCUS

Father, I know You made me on purpose. Of this, I am certain. I am here on purpose for You, to do Your will. My desire is to please You, to follow You and do whatever it is that You purposed for me.

My mind is open, my heart is willing and my body is able. Ever loving Father, I ask You to fill my spirit with Your Holy Spirit so that I may hear, see, do and speak what is pleasing to You.

JEREMIAH 42:3 NIV

"Pray that the LORD your God will tell us where we should go and what we should do."

NEXT STEPS: SHOW AND TELL

Over the last several weeks you have connected with the heart behind serving, identified some needs of the community and learned some practical ways you can use your gifts to meet those needs. This is just the beginning. Hopefully you have discovered your specific passions and identified a way that you can serve your community. Living out your Serve can be as simple as starting your own small group to meet that need.

Identify the **"WHAT"** .

There are a number of different ways you can make a difference in your community. Visit a nursing home, take meals to shut-ins, assist the disabled with small home repairs, tutor students or Serve at a food pantry—these are just a few ideas to get you inspired. The key is to build your small group around your gifts, passions and what God has put on your heart to do.

You can begin by asking yourself the following questions. Hopefully, the answers will help you launch or join a small group around your God-given purpose.

- What are you good at doing and love to do? *(Refer back to what you learned in the Discover Your Serve, Session 3.)*

- What individuals, ministries or organizations around you could benefit from your skills?

- What needs in your community seem to stand out to you above others?

Identify the **"WHO"** .

In forming a small group, we can learn from the apostles. They chose men who were:

1. Within their sphere of **INFLUENCE.** Who is in your circle of friends that you can invite to join your group?

2. Team **PLAYERS** : Who do you know that can contribute to your Serve?

Your small group isn't just about the people you're serving, but also about those serving alongside you. There are others around you who share your same interests. Consider inviting to the group those who you can mentor and encourage in their walk with Christ. As the leader it's important that you are pouring into those who are serving in your group.

> "Therefore, brethren, select from among you seven men of good reputation, full of the Spirit and of wisdom, whom we may put in charge of this task." (Acts 6:3 NAS)

TELL IT

Share your small group idea with your leader and discuss next steps.

....

....

....

....

....

....

....

....

....

....

....

....

....

....

SHOW IT

Recruit and share—tell everyone you know what you are doing. Your excitement will generate a response. Complete the requirements — find out what requirements your church has to lead a small group and begin completing them.

....
....
....
....
....
....
....
....
....
....
....
....
....
....
....
....
....
....
....

A FEW FINAL THOUGHTS...

....

....

....

....

....

....

....

....

....

....

....

....

....

....

....

....

....

....

....

....

....

....

....

....

....

ANSWER KEY

(PAGE NUMBERS BASED ON PARTICIPANT'S GUIDE)

WEEK ONE

Page 6
- God
- Form Relationships
- Sample
- Extra Mile
- Glorify

WEEK TWO

Page 11
- Spiritual Gifts
- Heart and Passion
- Abilities

Page 12
- Personality
- Experiences

WEEK THREE

Page 19
- Identify and Engage

Page 20
- Needs
- Resources

WEEK FOUR

Page 25
- Mandate
- People

Page 26

- Overcomers
- Local Church
- Poor
- Trust
- Consistent
- Confidential

Page 27

- Close
- Empathy
- Slow Down
- Questions
- Your Emotions
- Accommodate
- Needs
- Ideas
- Personalities

Page 28

- Faults
- Mission
- Goals
- Win
- Strengths and Weaknesses
- Roles and Tasks

WEEK SIX

Page 41

- Vision
- Roles

Page 42

- Timeline

WEEK SEVEN

Page 47

- What

Page 48

- Who
- Influence
- Players

ADDITIONAL
RESOURCES

TO ORDER COPIES OF THESE BOOKS
GO TO ARCCHURCHES.COM

DON'T DO MINISTRY ALONE.

It's not just about the mission, it's about the relationship we have with God and with each other. Whether you are looking to launch, connect or equip your church, ARC is for you.

WE ARE AN ASSOCIATION OF RELATIONAL CHURCHES WORKING WITH CHURCH PLANTERS AND CHURCH LEADERS TO PROVIDE SUPPORT, GUIDANCE, AND RESOURCES TO LAUNCH AND GROW LIFE-GIVING CHURCHES.

WE LAUNCH

We have a highly successful, proven model for planting churches with a big launch day to gain the initial momentum needed to plant a church. We train church planters, and we provide a tremendous boost in resources needed.

WE CONNECT

We provide dozens of opportunities to connect with other church planters, veteran pastors, leadership mentors, as well as friends who are walking the same path as you are. You're never short on opportunities to connect!

WE EQUIP

Our team continually creates and collects great ministry resources that will help you and your church be the best you can be. As part of this family, you get to draw water from a deep well of experience in ministry.

LAUNCHING, CONNECTING, & EQUIPPING THE LOCAL CHURCH

ARCCHURCHES.COM   *@ARCCHURCHES*   */WEPLANTLIFE*